James Dunn's family comes from Scotland, Ireland, England and Wales.
He grew up in the Scottish Highlands and lives in North London, where he works in publishing.
His favourite bits of the UK are the split rock at Clachtol in Sutherland, the maze at Tintagel in
Cornwall, Edinburgh in August and a restaurant called Moro in London. This is his first book.

Helen Bate is an exciting new illustrator and a qualified architect. She loves
the Isle of Mull in Scotland, Coventry and Ramsgate. She has illustrated
the *Purple Class* stories by Sean Taylor and *Sita, Snake-Queen of Speed*
by Franzeska G. Ewart for Frances Lincoln.

With thanks to Phoebe, Frances, Nigel and Sarah – J.D.
For Rachel, Alice and Hattie, with love – H.B.

ABC UK copyright © Frances Lincoln Limited 2008
Text copyright © James Dunn 2008
Illustrations copyright © Helen Bate 2008

First published in Great Britain in 2008 and in the USA in 2009 by
Frances Lincoln Children's Books, 4 Torriano Mews,
Torriano Avenue, London NW5 2RZ

First paperback edition published in 2009

www.franceslincoln.com

British Library Cataloguing in Publication Data available on request

ISBN: 978-1-84780-076-3

The illustrations for this book are mixed media

Printed in China

1 3 5 7 9 8 6 4 2

ABC UK

James Dunn

Illustrated by Helen Bate

F

FRANCES LINCOLN
CHILDREN'S BOOKS

A is for Arthur

B is for The Beatles

D is for Dragon

E is for Explorers

G
is for
Giant's Causeway

H
is for

Holmes

I is for Inventors

J is for
Jury

K is for Kilt

Llanfairpwllgwyngyllgogerychwyrndrobwllllantysiliogogogoch

M is for Mini

N is for Nessie

Q is for Queen

R is for Robin Hood

S is for Stonehenge.

T is for Tea

U is for Union Jack

A Taste of India restaurant and takeaway

V is for Vindaloo

W is for Wellies

X is
for
Kiss

Y is for Yorkshire Pudding

Z is for Zero Degrees Longitude

ALPHABET GLOSSARY

A

Arthur – A legendary king who defended Britain from invaders with the help of his queen Guinevere, the Knights of the Round Table and the magician Merlin. After a terrible last battle he was taken, wounded, to the magic isle of Avalon where he waits to return in Britain's hour of greatest need.

B

The Beatles – John, Paul, George and Ringo were four working class boys from Liverpool whose passionate and optimistic tunes made them the world's best loved rock-and-roll band.

C

Carnival – Europe's biggest street festival is held in London every August. It is a noisy, colourful celebration of Anglo-Caribbean culture with costumes, calypso, soca, steelpan and sound systems.

D

Dragon – You find dragons in Wales where they are a national symbol, in Chinatown for Chinese New Year parades and carved into the hill at Uffington where Saint George, the patron saint of England, is said to have fought a particularly unfriendly one.

E

Explorers – British people have been sailing off to explore the world for hundreds of years, from the Poles to the Arabian desert to the heart of Africa. The first person to write about exploring Britain was Pytheas, a Greek merchant who sailed round the British Isles more than two thousand years ago.

F

Football – Games of football have been played all over the world for hundreds of years. Association football or 'soccer' is the most popular team sport in the world, and follows the rules originally laid down in 1882 in Manchester.

G

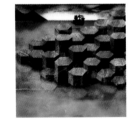

Giant's Causeway – An amazing natural rock formation in Antrim, Northern Ireland. The story goes that Finn McCool, an Irish giant, fell in love with a lady giant in Scotland, and he threw all these stones in the sea to make a bridge so that he could visit her.

H

Holmes – The famous fictional detective Sherlock Holmes uses his skills of observation and reasoning to solve seemingly impossible crimes from his home at 221b Baker Street in London.

I

Inventors – Inventors from the UK have benefited the world with inventions like penicillin, the telephone, the vacuum cleaner and the clockwork radio. It is said that two-fifths of all the patents granted throughout the world for new inventions in the last 50 years have been to inventors from the British Isles.

J

Jury – Twelve ordinary people (or fifteen in Scotland) decide in a trial if someone accused of a crime is guilty or not guilty. A jury helps to guarantee a fair trial, as the jurors do not know the accused, so they aren't on one side or the other to start with.

K

Kilt – A traditional outfit from the Highlands of Scotland. Each family has a different pattern, called a tartan. Never ask a Scotsman what he wears under his kilt!

L

Llanfairpwllgwyngyllgogerychwyrndrobwllllantysiliogogogoch – The name of a railway station in Wales. In English it means "The church of St Mary in the hollow of white hazel trees near the rapid whirlpool by St Tysilio's of the red cave". You roughly pronounce it *hlan-vier-poohl-guin-gill-go-ger-u-queern-drob-oohl-hlandus-ilio-gogo-gock*.

M

Mini - The most popular car ever made in the UK, the mini was very small and didn't use much petrol. They looked cute and they were good for nipping round old crooked streets.

N

Nessie - A mysterious monster living in the depths of Loch Ness in the Highlands of Scotland. There have been reports of sightings for over a thousand years, but no one knows for sure if the Loch Ness Monster actually exists.

O

Oak - The British Isles used to be covered by a great wild wood. The trees have mostly gone, though some beautiful forests remain. The oak leaf is the symbol of the National Trust, which protects special places in England, Wales and Northern Ireland.

P

Punk - In the 1970s, young people in Britain and worldwide were fed up with the lack of energy and ideals in the people running their countries. They expressed their feelings by dressing outrageously and making exciting music.

Q

Queen - The Queen has the job of representing the UK. Her picture is on our coins and stamps, and she works hard visiting people here and abroad.

R

Robin Hood - Living outside the law in Sherwood Forest with Maid Marian and the Merry Men, Robin Hood robbed from the rich to feed the poor.

S

Stonehenge - Four thousand years ago, British people dragged huge stones across the land, and arranged them to make Stonehenge. We don't know why they did it, but on midsummer morning the sun rises over the stones in a particular way, so perhaps it was a kind of gigantic calendar.

T

Tea – People in China have been drinking tea for about five thousand years. As British people started to trade with China three hundred years ago we got a taste for it too and now it's the nation's favourite drink – in the morning with breakfast, in the afternoon with cake or whenever it's time for a good chat.

U

Union Jack – The UK's flag is a mixture of England's red cross of St George, Scotland's white diagonal cross of St Andrew and Ireland's red diagonal cross of St Patrick (though, since 1921, only Northern Ireland is part of the UK). There's no Welsh dragon because Wales was already united with England when the flag was created 400 years ago.

V

Vindaloo – Portuguese traders invented this dish in Goa on the Western coast of India hundreds of years ago. British people call spicy food from this part of the world 'curry' and we eat lots of it!

W

Wellies – The UK is a collection of islands on the edge of the Atlantic Ocean, and all that water means that it rains quite a lot. Waterproof Wellington boots make splashing in puddles much more fun!

X

X (kiss) – Some of the most wonderful love stories in the world come from Britain, from Tristan and Iseult to Romeo and Juliet to John Smith and Pocahontas to Darcy and Elizabeth to Bridget Jones and Darcy.

Y

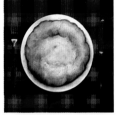

Yorkshire Pudding – a delicious thing to eat with roast beef, which is a traditional Sunday Lunch. It's made with flour, eggs, milk and the juice of the meat as it cooks.

Z

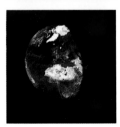

Zero Degrees Longitude – Every place in the world measures its position by how many degrees East or West it is of Greenwich in London, which is at zero degrees longitude. This was agreed in 1884, because by then most people were using this system already.

MORE PAPERBACKS FROM FRANCES LINCOLN CHILDREN'S BOOKS

We are Britain!
Benjamin Zephaniah
Photographs by Prodeepta Das

Poems about 13 children who come from a whole range
of cultural backgrounds all over Britain. Written by cutting-edge
performance poet Benjamin Zephaniah and full of photos and
facts, this is the rhyming, rapping, rhythmic way to learn
about Britain in the 21st century!

W is for World
Kathryn Cave
In association with Oxfam

From Alfredo in Mozambique to Zoe in Jamaica, take a glimpse at
the lives of children across the globe in this photographic
alphabet book. Featuring over 20 countries from Greenland to
Vietnam, it shows how many things people of different
backgrounds have in common.

Let's Eat!
Children and their Food Around the World
Beatrice Hollyer
In association with Oxfam

What we eat says a lot about where we come from. The children
in this book live in very different countries, and they each have
their own ideas about what tastes good. But they have lots in
common, too: they all go food shopping and help with the
cooking; share mealtimes with their families; eat special foods to
celebrate; and have things they love to eat and things they don't.

Frances Lincoln titles are available from all good bookshops. You can also buy books and find out more about
your favourite titles, authors and illustrators on our website: www.franceslincoln.com